SOCIAL STUDIES MATTERS!

WHAT IS HISTORY?

PETER FINN

PowerKiDS press

Published in 2024 by The Rosen Publishing Group, Inc.
2544 Clinton Street, Buffalo, NY 14224

First Edition

Editor: Therese Shea
Book Design: Michael Flynn

Photo Credits: Cover, p. 1 AlexAnton/Shutterstock.com; (series background) Eky Studio/Shutterstock.com; p. 5 nito/Shutterstock.com; p. 7 Merydolla/Shutterstock.com; p. 9 https://commons.wikimedia.org/wiki/File:Cleric-Knight-Workman.jpg; p. 11 https://en.wikipedia.org/wiki/File:Thure_de_Thulstrup_-_L._Prang_and_Co._-_Battle_of_Gettysburg_-_Restoration_by_Adam_Cuerden.jpg; p. 13 Aleksandr Stezhkin/Shutterstock.com; p. 15 W. Scott McGill/Shutterstock.com; p. 17 Frame Stock Footage/Shutterstock.com; p. 19 Everett Collection/Shutterstock.com; p. 21 BearFotos/Shutterstock.com.

Library of Congress Cataloging-in-Publication Data

Names: Finn, Peter, 1978- author.
Title: What is history? / Peter Finn.
Description: Buffalo, New York : PowerKids Press, [2024] | Series: Social studies matters! | Includes bibliographical references and index.
Identifiers: LCCN 2023037386 (print) | LCCN 2023037387 (ebook) | ISBN 9781499443981 (library binding) | ISBN 9781499443974 (paperback) | ISBN 9781499443998 (ebook)
Subjects: LCSH: History–Philosophy–Juvenile literature.
Classification: LCC D16.8 .F56 2024 (print) | LCC D16.8 (ebook) | DDC 901–dc23/eng/20230826
LC record available at https://lccn.loc.gov/2023037386
LC ebook record available at https://lccn.loc.gov/2023037387

Manufactured in the United States of America

CONTENTS

It's in the Past 4
Civilizations 6
Times and Places 8
Events 10
How We Know 12
Searching for Evidence 16
True or Not? 18
We Are History 20
Glossary 22
For More Information 23
Index 24

It's in the Past

History is the study of the human past. That sounds simple, right? But think of *everyone* who has lived. Think of *everything* that has happened. This is all history! People who study history are called historians. They write the history that we learn about.

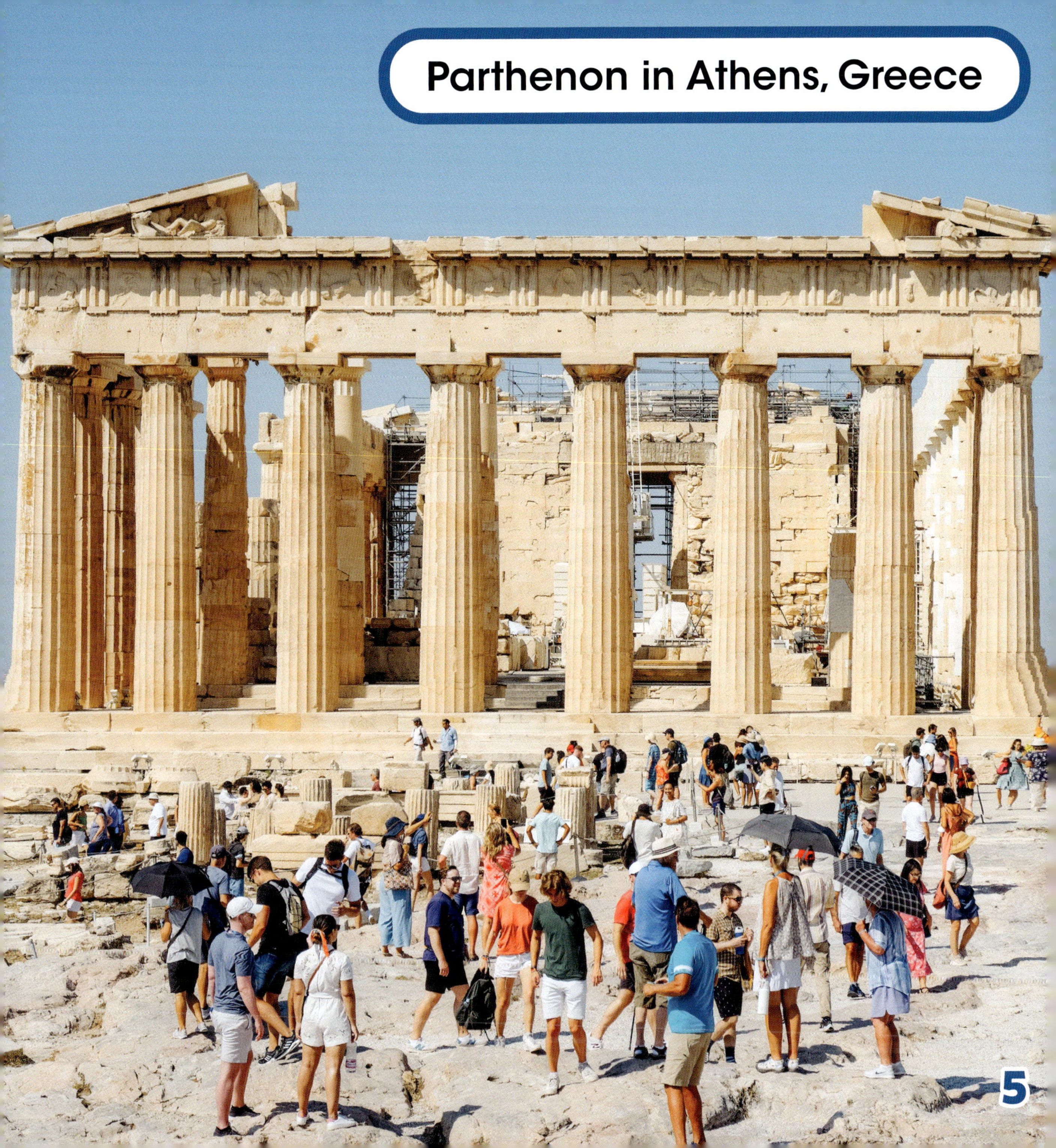

Parthenon in Athens, Greece

Civilizations

Some historians study **civilizations** from long ago. Egyptian civilization began in North Africa about 5,000 years ago. Rulers called pharaohs ruled for thousands of years. The **ancient** Egyptians left behind objects, such as the **pyramids**. These are clues about their **culture**.

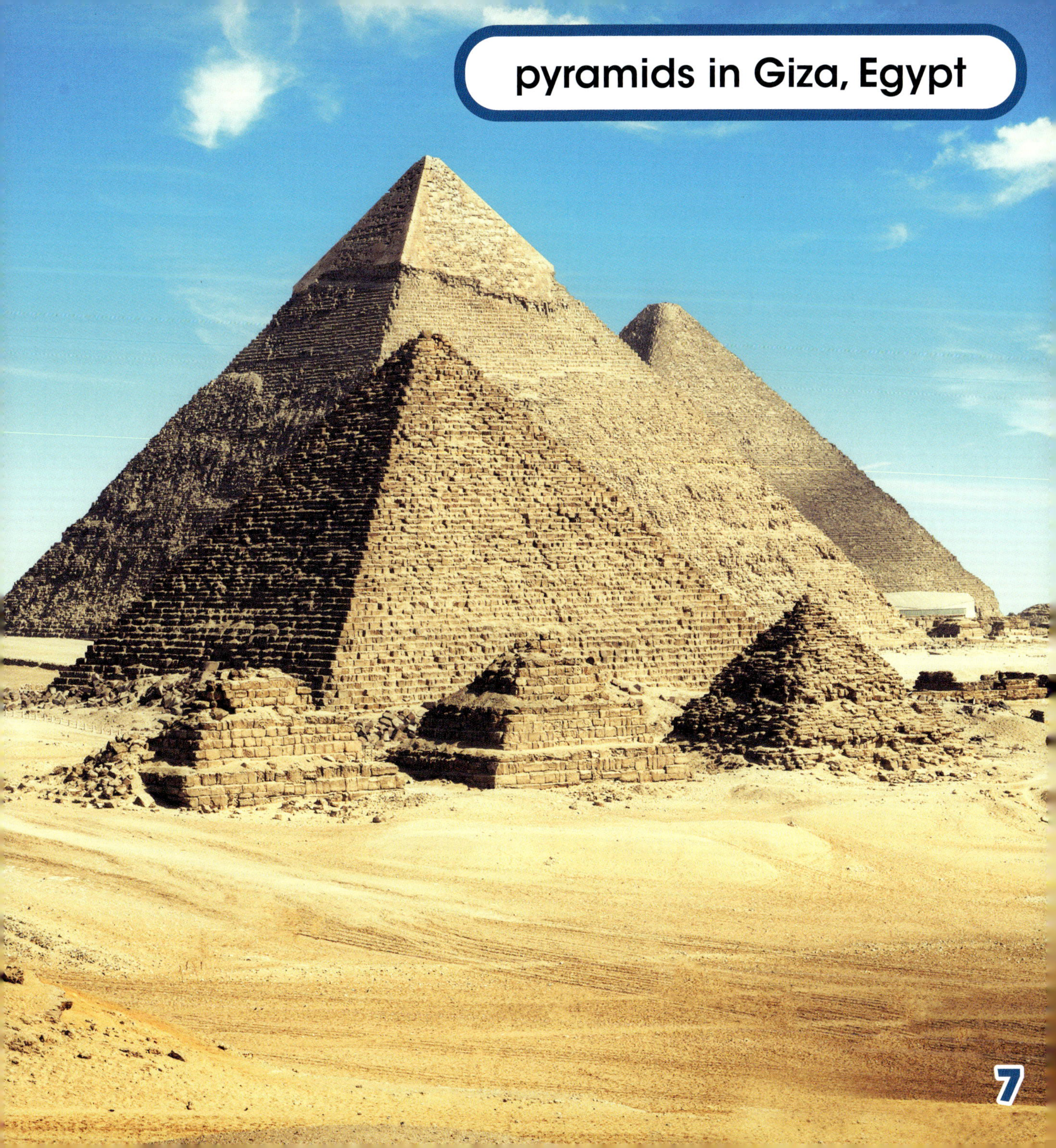

pyramids in Giza, Egypt

Times and Places

Some historians **focus** on a certain time or place. The Middle Ages is the name of a period of history in Europe. It lasted from about 500 **CE** to about 1500 CE. Writings and art from the Middle Ages tell us about life back then.

Events

Some historians study an event. The American Civil War was fought between the Northern United States and Southern states. It lasted from 1861 to 1865. Historians study leaders' **decisions** and the results of those decisions. They also read soldiers' journals and letters.

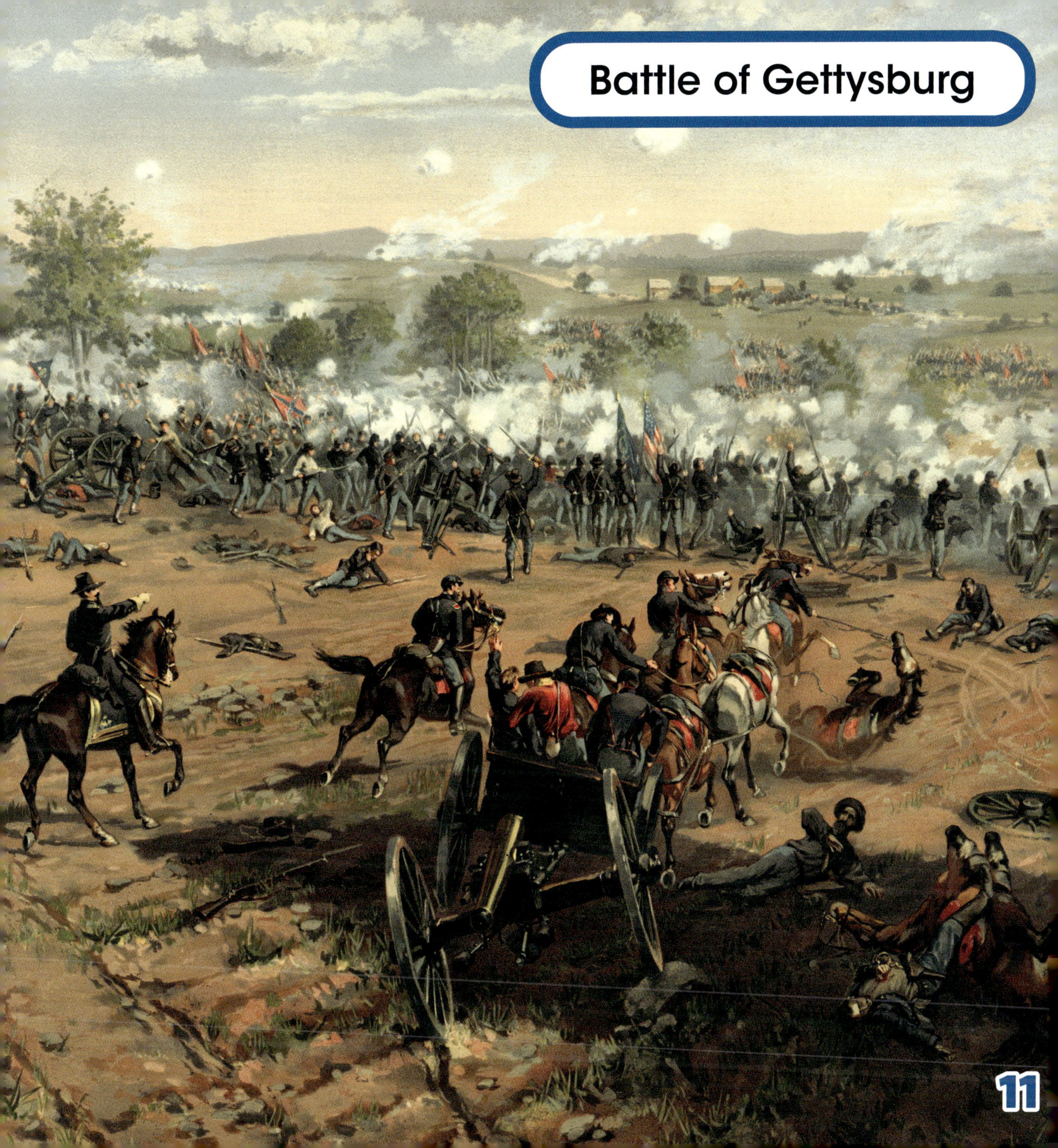

Battle of Gettysburg

How We Know

Historians use evidence, or clues, to find out what happened in the past. Writings are important evidence. The first writing system was invented about 5,000 years ago in **Mesopotamia**. Different kinds of writing followed in Egypt, China, the Americas, and other places.

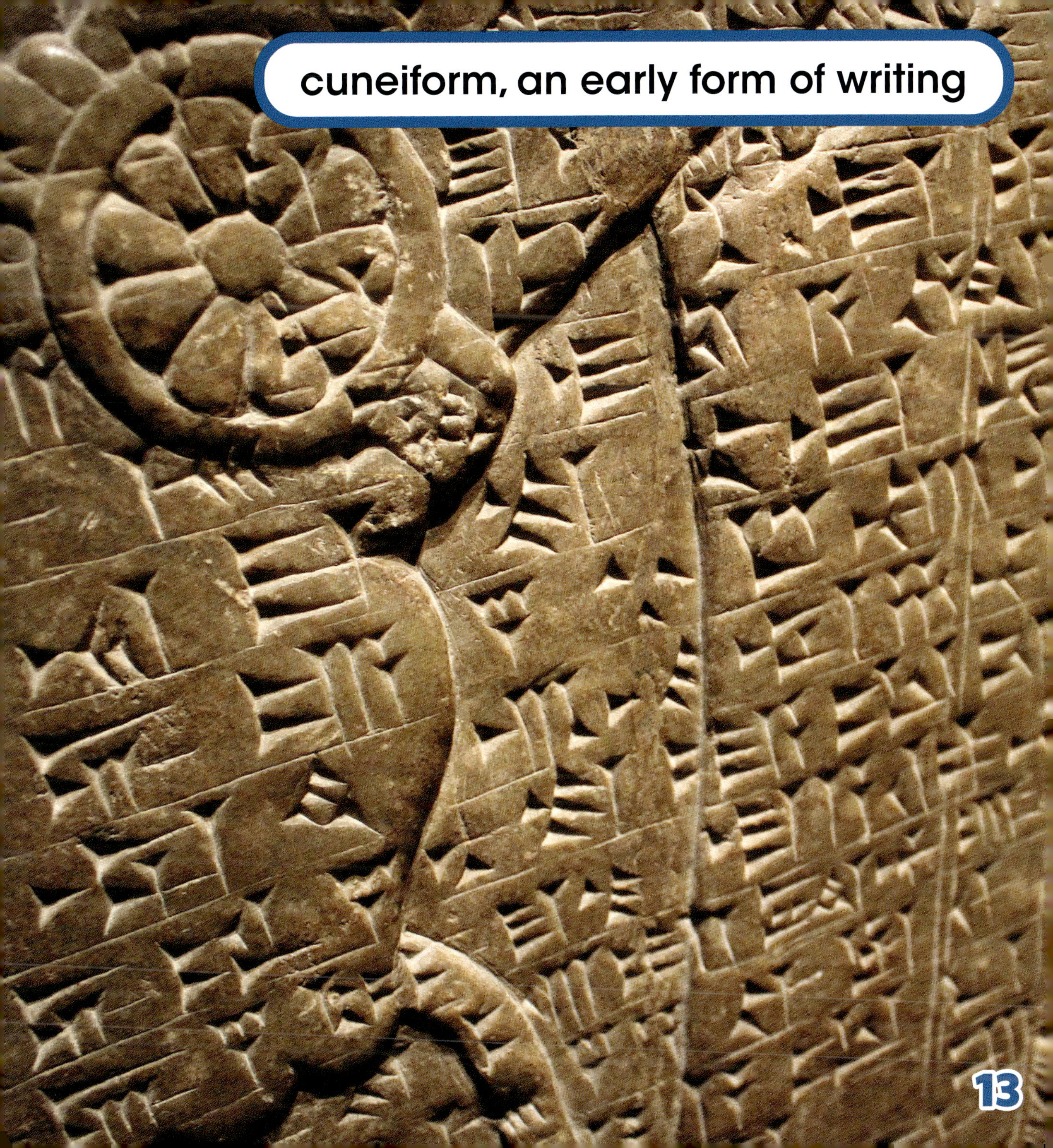

cuneiform, an early form of writing

Historians use writings such as letters, books, journals, and newspapers to understand history. Knowledge of history also comes from things such as tools, maps, photos, paintings, and other art. All these are primary sources. They were made by people who lived during a time or event.

Native American arrowheads

Searching for Evidence

Finding primary sources can be hard. Some have been partly or totally destroyed over the years. Others have been lost. Some are buried. Scientists called archaeologists look for artifacts, or objects made by humans. They often dig in the ground to find them.

True or Not?

Historians have to look at evidence carefully. They try to find out what's true. Some writings have parts that aren't true. A biography, or life story, of George Washington said he chopped down his father's cherry tree. Historians discovered this never happened!

We Are History

You learn history in school. You can learn history in **museums** too. The past helps us understand the present. Many laws, holidays, and other practices come from the past. History can help us understand other cultures as well. Today's events will become history too!

GLOSSARY

ancient: From a very long time ago.

CE: Short for "Common Era." Used to talk about the years after Jesus Christ is said to have been born. BCE means "Before the Common Era."

civilization: Organized society with written records and laws.

culture: The beliefs and ways of life of a group of people.

decision: A choice made about something after thinking about it.

focus: To direct your attention or effort to something.

Mesopotamia: An area of Western Asia between the Tigris and Euphrates Rivers.

museum: A building in which things of interest are displayed.

pyramid: A building that has a square base and four triangular sides that form a point at the top.

FOR MORE INFORMATION

BOOKS

Manzanero, Paula. *The Who Was? History of the World.* New York, NY: Penguin Workshop, 2021.

York, M. J. *History*. Mankato, MN: The Child's World, 2021.

WEBSITES

History
kids.britannica.com/kids/article/history/391022#
Learn more about how historians uncover history.

History for Kids
historyforkids.org/
Are you interested in a certain part of history? Check out these links.

INDEX

A
American Civil War, 10
Americas, 12
archaeologists, 16
art, 8, 14
artifacts, 16

C
China, 12
cultures, 6, 20

E
Egypt, 12
Egyptians, 6
Europe, 8

M
maps, 14
Mesopotamia, 12
Middle Ages, 8
museums, 20

P
paintings, 14
photos, 14
primary sources, 14, 16

T
tools, 14

W
Washington, George, 18
writings, 8, 12, 14, 18
writing system, 12